Just Words

Pamela Knight

Just Words © 2023 Pamela Knight

All rights reserved.

No part of this publication may be reproduced, stored in a retrieval system, or transmitted, in any form or by any means, electronic, mechanical, photocopying, recording, or otherwise, without the prior written permission of the presenters.

Pamela Knight asserts the moral right to be identified as the author of this work.

Presentation by *BookLeaf Publishing*

Web: www.bookleafpub.com

E-mail: info@bookleafpub.com

ISBN: 9789357610360

First edition 2023

DEDICATION

To my sister and friends, who all listened patiently to my poetic attempts

Sisters

Sister love and birthday hugs.
Spontaneous joy, hold tight.
Arms entwined, a perfect fit.
Legs fly, one snuggled up, one snuggled down.
True hearts roam, connect, sister love.

A Word

A word, your word
A single syllable to guide
Space, pause, simplify.
Motivation to appear or stillness defines
A synapse to tickle, to discover the reset.
A strange dimension,
Brings mind-bending thoughts.
Return to you, to your inner feels and allow the
flow, as tangents diverge.

My Lap

Chair, bed, floor, tent, only a moment for each.
Little ones edge gently forward.
Safety, comfort, love, final destination,
my lap.

Shitass

Another shitass day
Mother Nature is pissed
Maybe brain fog like the rest of us.
Day 39
It's spring not winter, we want out!
A breath of fresh warm air, a window flung open
What is this 21st-century crisis,
that brings weight gain as collateral damage.
How insane, how privileged, how unfathomable
Who are we?
But we stay in, saving lives,
this is considered hard work, REALLY?
It amazes me that the whole world is struggling
together but not the same.
I have space,
I have food,
I have water to wash my hands.
A RIGHT, not available to all.
I hope it brings us a better world when the
curtain lifts.

Where?

Where is our unity,
openness in our hearts, thoughts and deeds?
Time to strip the world bare and begin again,
Where is our humanity wizard?

Tea

Mint, chai or lemon ginger,
a calm in your day.
A peaceful beginning or a nighttime ritual
An early morning pleasure, slows me down, cheers
me up.
Unite mind, body and soul,
creating time for wandering thoughts.
Knowing another cup is around the zig or zag of
time.

Water, boil, fresh lemon, brings me a little bit of
heaven.
It's a place to start, to end or the in-between.
To sip and stare, to sip and contemplate, to sip and
scheme.
Whatever fits that space created by a cup of tea.

Darkness

I held your box of darkness for far too long.
I gave you that gift, I cared for the intertwined
mess created by two.

Neglect, lies, omissions.
Missed opportunities, expectations stamped
upon, never delivered.

Love lost in the quagmire of deceit.
Trust dissolves and anger fills the space.
I did the best I could,
Did you?

Alone

One day, I choose to be alone.
Just to become quiet,
to read, to ponder, to escape.
A moment in time,
loved ones question, "are you all right?"
Odd to take this whole moment,
just for me.

Lake Tangamong

Sun stretches her arms,
Curl of the water ripples,
Fairies alight with a sprinkling of kinetic motion.
My eyes delight as thousands of wings create a dance
upon the crest.
Air creates the sudden wave of the leaves,
reflecting light and shapes onto the undulating
current,
My senses absorb a perfect synchronicity of nature.

Take this Step

All I can do is share a title, a book, a thought.
My knowledge is not deep enough to inform, to
teach, to assess.
I want to create a space, a moment to pause and
reflect.
There are many layers to unfold.
So please take this step with me,
 to go inside, to see from another view.

Human

The world has lost its tick and doesn't know how
to navigate the tock,
minutes, hours, years, decades.
Where is the deep change that is needed to
amass our collective kindness.
To create a new space, to just be human.

Truth

Sadness sits heavy, my walls dissolve, thoughts
have no place to settle.
Afraid to speak the truth, as the minutes pass,
those truths do too.
Questioning what is in my heart, my psychology,
my inner being.
Are they one, or scattered like the fall leaves,
impossible to reassemble the majestic tree?
Does each new beginning, each new motion,
bring a subtle shift?
Or is it just a game I play as I try to decipher
who I really am?

Death

Death, memories, foibles fall away,
pedestal is erected.

anger
grace
connections
your choice
your memories

perspective
peace
mind chatter released
seek calm within the inner world, the outer
world moves forward.

Southampton

Water, sand, forest,
clouds swelling my creative power.
Summer getaways
Sweet friends
Delightful sustenance
Stories to share.

Evergreen, deciduous and ferns
Define the walking path.
Upward a peek of blue, below feet traverse the
trodden trail.
Rays of sunlight glistening, body awash in
wonder.

Forest opens, focus drawn upward, clouds
mesmerize.
Shapes and patterns, shifting constantly. Shades
of the sky abound.

Nature can be kind, wild and cruel.
A walk through the gifts of our earth brings pure
joy to my being.

Little Ones

Three little ones connected
Gentle touches
sweet kisses
total wonder
Oldest, middle, youngest
Each one so individual
Sometimes tears erupt but sister love overcomes.

What do I Really Want

What truly makes me feel that inner joy,
 a smile rising from within?
Why can't I pinpoint the vision or even a cloudy
view?
So many paths that seem to be the fresh anew,
find the piece that fits just for me.
So many ideas, I watch others as their parts
connect to their whole.
Is that my avenue too?
I could do that!
But I am me,
can I find my door?

Clarify

I feel the ebb and flow, time seems to be waiting.
Waiting for me to clarify how this chapter will emerge.
Do I need a cataclysmic change or just a quiet redo?
Or maybe the global world at this precise moment in time is the force that has cracked open time and space for a rethink, a shift, in me and maybe in all.

Camping

Paddle, lake, narrows, lake
Tent up, fly secure
Mattress, all my air, dizzy moment
Bathing suit on, noodle at the ready, book in
hand, perfection
Blue sky, billowy character clouds, clear water,
pieces fitting perfectly, dive
Time is on your side, no diversions, mind free of
clutter, wood, pine needles, one match, fire, heat,
flames, crackle, mesmerizing.
Camping with my sister!

Motion

Morning thoughts awakening.
Imagery from nature leads to a metaphor for living.
Lily pads connected, glistening, rolling gently, seemingly free but beneath the ripple tied to one another.
An alien head, the eyes of a frog or maybe a hippo,
just skimming the water, as if synchronistically propelling the group forward.
Yet it is an illusion of motion, no real progress.
How often does one feel they are trying so diligently
Forward motion seems so alluring, at your fingertips, yet simultaneously so unattainable
I say to my lily pad team, my hippo, my alien head, my frog, keep trying, your moment will come.
Something will click and a smile will emerge, success is an option.
It's ok to believe in the power of yes.

Flow

What if I am on my path
What if I settle into this life I have
What if today is just right, exactly where I
should be
What if my hopes and dreams embrace me each
day
What if as my world unfolds around me, I learn
to marvel
What if contentment is allowed to permeate my
being
What if the guilt, the envy, the more, more,
more, dissipates like the mist on the early
morning Tangamong
The simple word enough is all encompassing
To have enough
To be enough
 To find your peace with your enough
This is life!

Brooke

Sweet surrender to the forces that surround
To the universe that guides
And the love that creates the space to conquer all
Soft needles of a forest walk or the steep ascent of a
mountain climb.

Your courage, your strength opens your being, where
your light emanates, giving you even more fortitude
to traverse the challenges.

Caress each moment with your positive spirit and
share your joy for the time spent within your circle.
Your life force connects to every fibre of those you
love and carries you as one,
separate but entwined.

Giving true self and receiving in return their true
hearts.
You are a trillion tiny fairy lights that you have
planted with your passions, never to extinguish,
always there to guide you and all those you have
nurtured through your gifts of love, time, joy,
laughter, resilience and strength.
You have, you do and you will continue on your
journey of making a difference
You are loved!

www.ingramcontent.com/pod-product-compliance
Lightning Source LLC
LaVergne TN
LVHW021349200726

843509LV00014B/2759

9 789357 610360